Bits and Pieces

Srushti Rao

BookLeaf
Publishing

Presentation by *BookLeaf Publishing*

Web: www.bookleafpub.com

E-mail: info@bookleafpub.com

ISBN:9789358734300

First edition 2023

To Dad.

I wish you were here.

ACKNOWLEDGEMENT

Everyone who has ever inspired me to feel, think, question and write. I am forever grateful that you were or are a part of my journey. All of me today is my life experiences put together, and I would not have it any other way. So thank you for your contribution. To the reader, thank you for being a part of this journey by reading my words. Eternally grateful for everything.

When the waves engulf you with the full fury of nature, you know how powerless you are against the will of nature. Precisely then, courage meets your tired limbs and pushes the boundaries of human frailty with the will to live and save something more precious than life itself.

Let Us Pretend

Let us pretend
Pretend to be each other's 'forever'
We know we aren't
We know we can't be
But, play this game with me
Humour me

Let us pretend
To love each other at our worst
When we can't even look at ourselves
Let us adore each other

Let us pretend
Pretend to be each other's 'forever'

'Be Mine' I tell you
You say 'Yes'
Let us pretend

When I say 'Run away with me'
You say 'Yes'
Let us pretend

When I say 'Will you love me with my flaws'
You say 'Yes'
Let us pretend

My forever can be a million years
Yours can be a few hours
But let it be a 'forever' nonetheless

Let us pretend
That your forever and mine are the same
Even if they aren't

Let us pretend
That we will survive this
Even if hope is leaving shore

Let us pretend
Fun, frolic and all things nice
even if the hurt is pricking

They say love can withstand the worst
Even if there is no scope left
Let us pretend
Pretend to be each other's 'forever'

He Loved Her

He loved her at her best
He loved her at her worst
He loved her when she was beautiful
He loved her when she was ugly

He loved her when she was sunshine
He loved her when she was thunderstorm
He loved her through the shades of white to
black
And the greys in-between

He loved her rainbow
He loved her overcast
He loved her every corner,
every curve and straight line

If I Go Away

If I go away
Will you come looking for me
Search me on the trails
we once walked

Ask for me
To the stars
We stared at and wondered

Run your fingers over the sand
We once built castles on
Dug our feet in till we couldn't feel them
anymore

Dip your feet in waters
That witnessed our kisses
Heard our sweet nothings

Will you come looking for me
If I go away

Love You Half-way

How can I love you half-way?
I don't know how
You told me why
But I still don't know how
I know how to love you only fully
boundlessly
completely
utterly
unabashedly
How do I not fall in love completely?
How do I hold back?
How do I love you half-way?

Even If Momentarily

You touched my soul
like the waves hit the sand
Even if you meant it momentarily

I stayed there
waiting
like the sand

Hoping for you to come back
Caress my presence
kiss my being
touch my soul

Once again
Even if momentarily

Allow Yourself

Feel everything
The good
The bad
The ugly
All of it

That's what the
human heart is made for
To feel

Allow yourself
To experience
The joy
The pain
The hurt
All of it

Allow yourself to feel
And then heal from it

It's beautiful

Life is a journey
Enjoy it
Live it
Feel it

A Full Heart

I loved you with a full heart
You picked on it
piece by piece
moment by moment
You broke it in pieces
One sharp edge at a time
till nothing was left

You took away pieces
Now my heart can never be full
I don't know what you did with those pieces
you took away

If you preserved them
Use them to heal someone else
I will make peace believing
someone else needed more healing than me

If you trashed them
I hope someone finds them
to heal themselves nonetheless

A full heart is rare to find
You had mine
So much so that
it could have healed yours

But you chose to walk away
with your broken heart
Breaking mine

I hope you don't break another full heart
They are rare to find

Piece By Piece

It will take me time
It will take me time to heal from this hurt
that you caused me
To gather the pieces

Some that you carelessly left behind
Some that you selfishly took along with you
Some strewn in places I fear to go back to
Some callously stashed in estranged territories

It will take me time to retrieve all pieces
Those very pieces I trustingly showed you

Introduced you to parts of me I was embarrassed
of
Pieces I preserved to share with someone who
would
nurture them
preserve them
value them

I will take time to stitch all of this together
To get my seamstress on
To tailor myself back in fashion

To be desirable first to myself
Let alone allow anyone else within

It will take me time to trust again
love again
To be uninhibited in my own skin

Where is It?

Where is the unabashed
fire of love
Where is the passion
Where is the ache
the desire
the torment
the urgency
the unexplained agony of love

Where is that great love
that philosophers warned us against
and poets wrote about

Where is that love
that builds you as it destroys you

Where is that love
which is both pleasure and pain

Or are these just stories
glorifying two miserable people together

Where is the love
that makes you conquer the world

Where is the love
that makes you love like never before

Where is the love
that unmistakably makes you desirable
and unapproachable at the same time

Where is the love
that burns through your entire existence
for this birth and the next
the love that you feel
you didn't exist before
and would cease to exist after

You write to me when you find it
cause I have ceased to exist

Unfair Ride

I fell hard
Harder than I intended
Harder than expected
Maybe I wasn't cautious enough
Not as cautious as you for sure

You didn't fall
You didn't even stumble
You just strung along
Dragging my fallen sorry behind along

It is an unfair ride
I am scathed
and you are upright
I am hurt from the wounds
You are strong in your strides

It is an unfair ride for sure
Now I know better
Not to fall
To stand upright
Not even to stumble
I may need crutches right now
But I will stand back up for sure
And maybe then I would be

far beyond your reach
far away with a strong stride

The Mind & Heart

My mind has travelled miles
Miles and miles
to be with you
It has travelled through
time
geographies
possibilities
destinies

My heart has clung on to the
hope of it all
It is all fun
till it is not

The mind confuses the heart
The battle between the two continues

The heart wants
what the mind knows it can't have
The mind continues
to charm the heart

The heart trusts it
till it knows better
The cycle continues

My Dreamland

Your are one elusive dream
that I hold on to
every night
Sleep has never been so dear to me than now
Every night when I close my eyes
You slide into my dreams
I get to hold you
be with you
love you
Tell me what better place to be
than that

If I Let You Go

If I let you go
would you find me again
would you return to me
If I let you be on your own
Would you be reminded of me
Would my love pull you back

If I cut this cord
Would you try to know the edges
Would you find joy in me again

If I let you go
Would you come back to me?

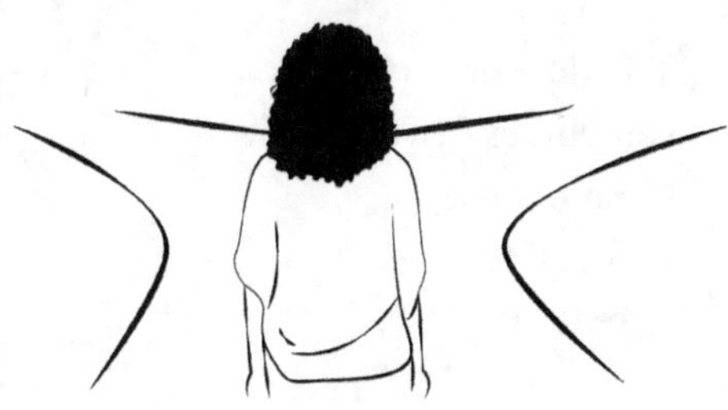

What Are You

You came into my life
when I wasn't even looking

You came in as my calm
But you are my chaos

I oscillate between the two
you being my calm
you being my chaos

What are you truly?
That peace that I seek
Or the impetus I crave

You devour my senses
sometimes my capability
to rationalise
to imagine
to reason

What are you truly?
my beginning
or my end

I Will Bounce Back

This is me expressing myself
Telling you how I feel
alone, deserted, unwanted
You have the clear path to walk away

This is me being
emotional, vulnerable
You can walk away with your logical mind

I won't be okay
But I will manage myself
I will cry, sulk, disappear

But when I come back
I will be healed
Shiny and sparkly as new
bedazzling the world
with my strength
despite the plethora of weaknesses
you see inside of me

You can walk away
You will break me
But I will bounce back
Shiny and sparkly as new

The Universe is Smiling

Sigh! What do I say?
I am lost for words
Poured them all out
Too soon, I wonder
Your weren't ready yet
Nor was I
But it needed to be said
You needed to know
Even though this silence is deafening
I know the Universe is smiling

It has plans
I know it does
It always does
It comes back to me eventually
Perhaps you will tide along
Perhaps you won't
We wouldn't know
Until the Universe has spoken

Ah! This silence is deafening
And maybe rightly so
All that was meant to be said
Was said
The words were all mine
The actions were yours
Loud nonetheless

Oh! This silence is deafening
But defining nonetheless
Your path and mine
Would they converge
Or would they diverge
Only the Universe can tell
And I know it is smiling

Lust for Life

I like myself a little more now
I look at my scars and smile
They remind me of the battles I fought
And the wounds that healed

They aren't all healed yet
It would take time
But I like myself a little bit more now
Every time one wound heals and becomes a scar

Scars are worn by warriors and fighters
And I will continue
No matter what
It isn't the lust for the war
Or the fight
Nope
It is not

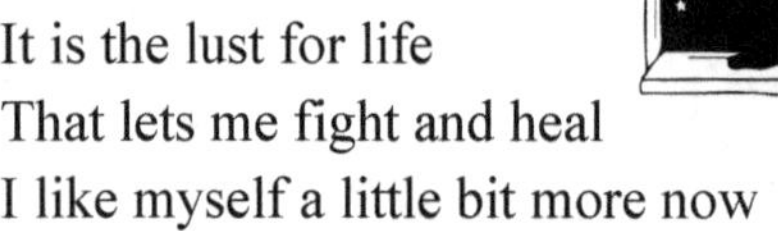

It is the lust for life
That lets me fight and heal
I like myself a little bit more now

One Breath at a Time

Did you miss me at all
all this while?
Or did you celebrate the
absence of sunshine?

I gave you too much power
The power to wield your will on me
I am taking it back now
Slowly
Yet steadily
One tiny breath at a time

I thought I could brighten
your darkness
But instead I dimmed my light
And yes, that was unfair to me
To the universe
That has assigned me to shine

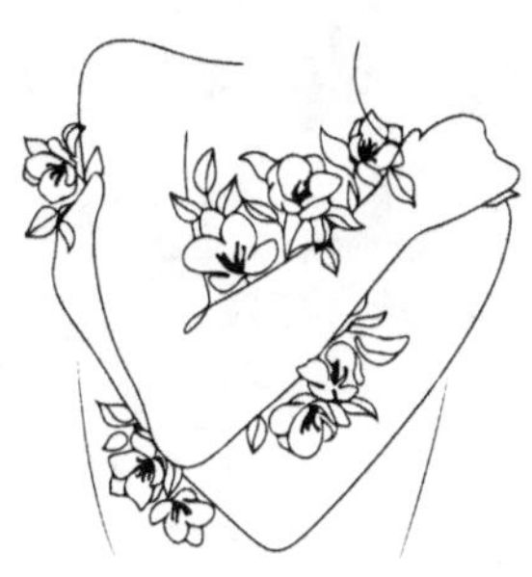

And shine I would
Brighter than you found me
Slowly
Yet steadily
One tiny breath at a time

I would again shine light
And you can then come
So I could brighten
some of your darkness
But never again
Am I dimming my own light

I will embrace you
I will love you
But this time the terms would be mine
One breath at a time

Remember

Remember when you
Played with my fingers
When we held hands
That, my love, is love

Remember when you
Tucked strands of my hair
Behind my ears
Because you couldn't see my eyes
When I was talking
That, my love, is love

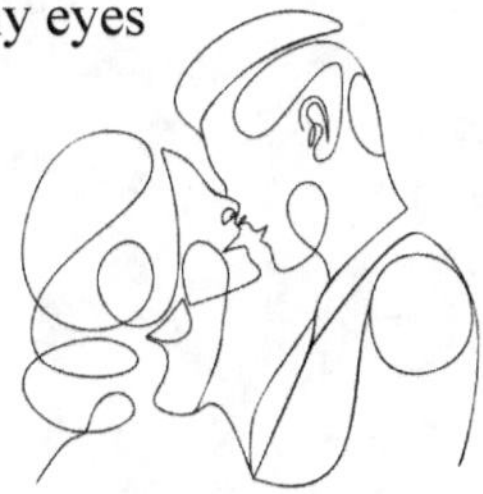

Remember when you
Tapped on my back
To ask me if I was okay
Because I had it turned to you
That, my love, is love

Remember when you
Brought me my favourite food
Because I was mad at you
That, my love, is love

No, I don't want the Sun
Or the Moon or the Seven Seas

I just want you to remember
The small things
And whisper sweet nothings
To play with my fingers
And tuck strands of my hair
That, my love, is love

Safe Space

Sitting in a corner
Anxious
Breathing heavily
I wonder how life was simpler before
When it wasn't about seeing you
Talking to you
Missing you
Meeting you

Life is complex now
And I allowed it
Surrendering to the matters of the heart
I knew better
But I let the heart lead the way

Travelled the ups and downs
The highs and lows
And the winding roads
Exhausted
Anxious
Breathing heavily
I wonder how life was simpler before

It would be wonderful to get some respite
But again

You are the respite
Your voice
Your touch
Your smile
Is my safe space

You make me feel
Protected
Taken care of
You are my calm
You are my safe space

Meet Me Half-Way

I have played these conversations
with you
multiple times in my head
I reason with you
You debate with me
I reason back
We argue some more
And then we settle

The truth is that it is all a lie
A make believe world
Created with real people and real feelings

I replay these conversations
And then we argue some more
But every time you come back to me

We find a middle ground
I don't ask for too much
And you give a little more

I can be little less greedy
You can be a little less detached
I replay it again in my head
The truth is that it is all a lie

A make believe world
Created with real people and real feelings

But none of this is unreal
Not you
Not me
May be one day
I can ask for a little more
And you will give a lot more
May be one day
You will meet me half-way

Believe

Hey you!
Yes, you.
I want to tell you something
You are doing better than most
You have more than most
You can create more than most
You are ok
You will be better
From here on
Trust yourself
Believe in yourself
You don't need them to tell you - You are
beautiful
Cause you are
You don't need them to tell you, you can do it
Cause you can
Breath in and believe

My Imagination

The power of imagination is wonderful
I can make you a star one day
The glorious Sun on some or the soothing Moon
on others
You are right there in front
And the most beautiful of things
Is the combination of creativity and imagination
I can make you a flower and preserve you in
these pages
To seek comfort when I want
I can see you in the raindrops as you nourish the
earth
And feel my soul touched
I can imagine you in a cold breeze
Imagine you swirling around me
I can imagine you in my flesh and bones
coursing through my being
You are everywhere for me yet nowhere
Maybe another lifetime
Maybe another universe
You are around and not just as a star, or the
moon or a flower

Let Us Create Butterflies

Let us recreate the butterflies
The fluttering in the stomach
The anticipation
The stolen glances
The accidental touches
The drifting conversations
Let us recreate viridity
The first touch
The first kiss
Yes, the first kiss
We know too much now
But how can we match the first kiss
Let us recreate everything that drew us together
Every now and then
Create novelty
There is too much to know
We haven't shared the inner layers yet
Let us create-recreate
Let us give space to butterflies

Endless Conversations

You think I write for you
I suppose I do
But honestly
I think I write for myself
To say things I cannot
To have conversations I cannot
In my writings you speak to me
You respond
You hold my head between your hands and we
talk endlessly sometimes
You praise
You critique
You love
You believe
So I write
To speak with you sometimes endlessly between
these limited lines

Meet Yourself

Meet me when you've
Met yourself
Discover me when you've discovered yourself
Explore my mind
When you've explored yours
When you are in touch with yourself
You will be able to reach places within me that
aren't apparent
When you've accessed your innermost demons
You would be able to deal with mine
When you've laughed with yourself silly
We can laugh together
When you have tuned in to your soul
Mine is yours to love

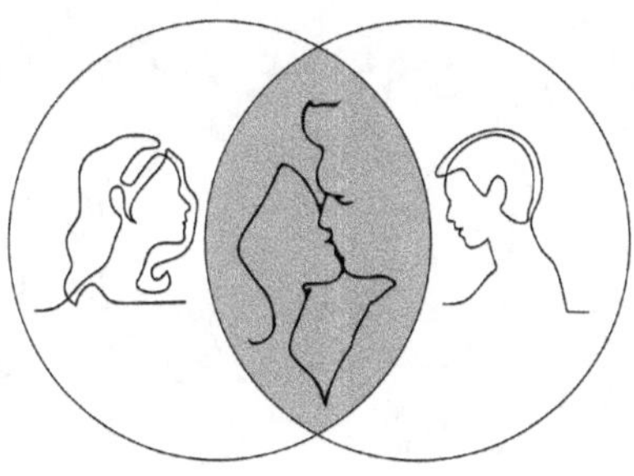

Stalemate

The old school me &
The new age me often argue
The old school me wants to hold on
The new age me wants to let go
The that me wants to put in the work
The this me wants to get rewarded soon enough
That me values patience
This me wants stuff done
The waiting fights with the wanting
Sometimes one wins over the other
Most times there is a stalemate
So I end up patiently wanting to get rewarded
soon enough

Is it Love

You say the lesser my expectations the more
comfortable you are
But that isn't love, is it?
Love is accepting each other in our extremities
The good, the bad, and the ugly
Is it love even, if only one of us is comfortable?
And the other is wondering
Why is this even?

One Day

When we meet next
Let us do one thing
Let us live & love one day
That's for me
And the next for you
Perhaps you can take all the other days
Let's make memories & Love on this day
It will last me a lifetime
A lifetime of smiles
A lifetime of you
A lifetime of feeling loved

Just Stop

Listen, just stop
If you aren't going to do anything about it
Stop making me fall in love with you
Stop making my heart race
And my pupils dilate
Stop popping in my head
Every now and then
Stop being the face of every romantic dream
I ever have
Stop featuring in every romantic song I ever hear
Stop being the fragrance I crave to breathe
everyday
Stop being magical
If you are not going to do anything about it
Just stop being the very essence of my existence

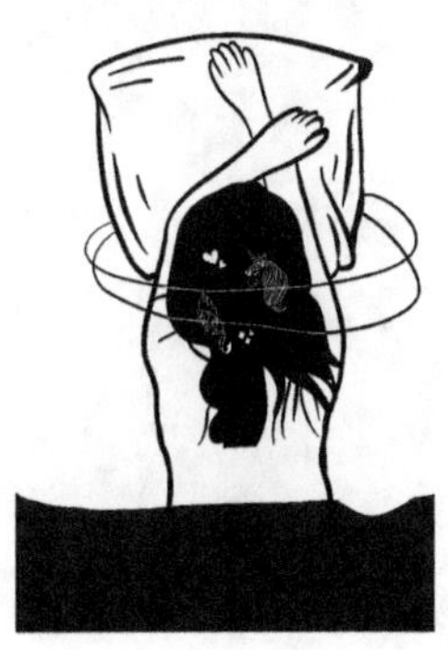

Gold and Diamond

Gold's softness
Diamond's hardness
Create exquisite
Pieces of jewellery
One needs both
the softness of love
the hardness of protection
to create a love that balances us
Our existence
Keeps us safe and cared for
You and I can create exquisite pieces

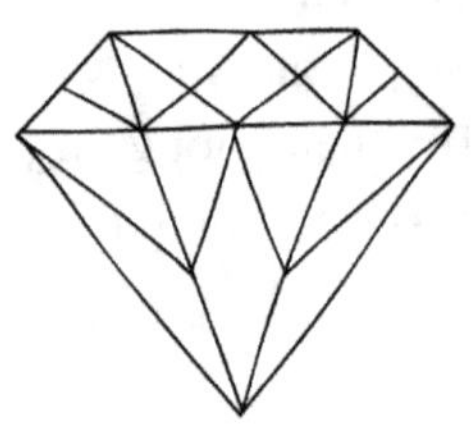

The Wait

You probably don't realise between the Hello there!
And the Goodbye
You leave behind
Countless glances at the blank screen
Excited leaps of the heart
When the phone buzzes
A million pieces of a broken heart when it's not you at the other end
A trail of broken promises
Countless conversations
That could have been
Lost smiles that could have turned into laughter
Untold stories that would be forgotten
Myriad dreams that could have been shared
Immeasurable delight
And oodles of unexpressed love

Let's Talk

I want to tell you everything
My joys, my sorrows
My wins, my losses
My comforts, my fears
I want you to walk with me in the lanes &
by-lanes of my mind
I want to invite you to the nooks & crannies of
my heart
I want you to know what still hurts
And what's healed
And I want to experience all that is yours too
Your hidden spaces
Your preserved moments
I want to see it all
I want to feel it all
I want to then hold you till we breathe as one

Too Much Love

Love is not just about giving in
It is also about receiving it
Did I give you too much love too soon?
Should I have rationed it a little bit for everyday
A dash here and a dash there
It could have lasted a little more
Or would it have truly?
Is too much love too soon even a thing?
Should we have calibrated our capacities for the
love dose?
No we shouldn't have since when does love have
SOPs
Or should love now be defined by a process
'This works for me'
'That's too much'
Oh please! Let love be love
Let it be free flowing
Like all things natural
Maybe I overwhelmed you
But I still think destiny beckons us
We would only know when it's over or it's all
over
Either ways we will know
But maybe I will love you a little less each day
So that it is not too much love too soon

Never Again

Never again would I be able to love so fearlessly
as I did you
Never again would I be able to present a pure
heart as it was
Never again would I be able to trust with sheer
love
Never again would I expose my most vulnerable
side to be
Punched and bruised

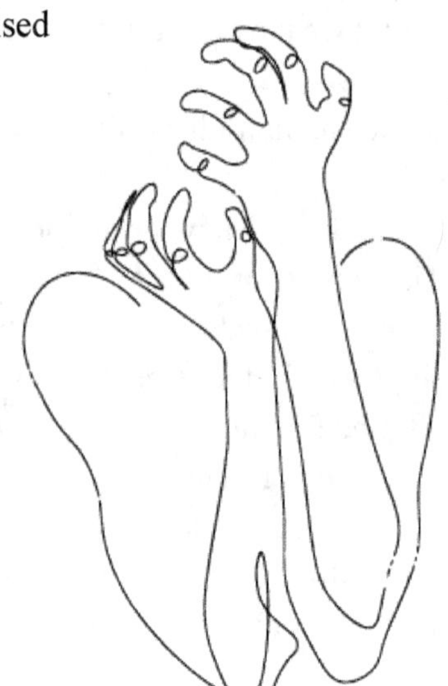

Serendipity

My eyes locked with yours
Like we knew each other
We didn't
You instigated me to smile
Without uttering a word
That was new
The affinity
The attraction
The familiarity
We knew each other but didn't know each other
at all
I was pulled towards you, magnetically
An unexplained power
An unexplained connection
Like we had ongoing conversations
But we didn't
Like we had said so much but so much was yet
to be said
Like we didn't need to introduce ourselves
We already connected
Did our souls find each other

To finish unfinished business
Did our souls meet in previous lifetimes
Do I owe you some love
Do you owe me some care
Are we here today reconciling an ongoing ledger
I had no reason to meet you in this lifetime nor
did you
But what is this energy that pulls us together
Now, then & forever

A Child

I want to be a child with you
Unreasonable
Demanding
I am tired of this grown-up stuff
Being the same
Making decisions
Why can't I just be stupid for once
Not thinking of the consequences
Not being careful
Not being calculative
And yet know
It will be okay
I want to be a child with you
I want to feel
Protected
Taken care of
Loved
No matter
What I say or do
I want to fight and cry and throw tantrums
And still be held close to the heart
Not judged
Not told to behave
I want to run, skip & jump
Without a care in the world
And still be loved

I want to be a child with you
To be loved unconditionally
Whether I am good or bad.

People Go Away

People value people only when they are gone
No more within reach
Everything that they offer as love
Companionship, advice, laughter & joy
Is otherwise taken for granted
Love them before they go away
Value them before they disappear
You would be lucky if you get another chance
Most often than not people don't get that
opportunity
Once gone, people don't come back
Love them before they are gone
Value them before they disappear

Resolve

Sometimes it takes a whole lot of strength to
cross a tiny puddle
Sometimes it takes just a little bit of courage to
cross the ocean
We have our good days and bad
We find anchors to plant our hopes to
We find reserves to draw strength from
To jump across the puddle or swim through the
ocean
The resolve is always within
We just need to tap into it
Awaken it each day
Be grateful
And keep on going

Rolled in One

You are my strength
And you are my weakness
You are my sunny day
And you are my cloudy night
You have the strength to make me believe
You have the power to break me into pieces
No one ever should be made so important
But there you are
My builder and my destroyer rolled in one

Hopeless Romantic

I am a hopeless romantic
Life hasn't been able to teach me a lesson yet
Cosy dinners, long drives, walk on the beach,
Still give me butterflies
Grazing lips, holding hands, intimate smiles,
Still make my heart skip a beat
I still believe in the pureness of love
That no-matter-what it exists
No matter how many times you have
experienced otherwise
It will find you
Pillow fights, endless tickles, footsies
Still light my fire
An arm around the waist, a whisper in the ear,
A kiss on the forehead
Still make me weak in my knee
I am a hopeless romantic and I hope life lets me
be

You are!

You are my beginning
and my end
You are my hope
and my despair
You are my gain
and my loss
You are my joy
and my sorrow
You are everything to me
Yet you are nothing at all
You are my realisation
You are my contradiction

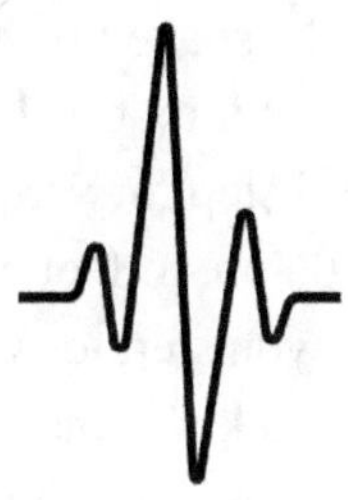

Letting Go

Right here, right now
I am letting you go
Old wisdom says
The tighter you hold the sand
The faster it slips
But it slips anyway
So yes, even if I want to hold on to you
With all my might
I am letting you go
Not just for me for you too
I am letting you go
To make space for growth
To make space to learn
For me not to look back
When I step forward
For you not to feel pulled back
When you step forward
For us to know that
Letting go is not the end of our story
For me to understand
That letting go can also mean to let it be

Dear Fate

I met two versions of you
One was my dream come true
And the other seemed askew
One version loved back intensely
The other hesitated to bare it all
I could feel the depth of emotion
Contrarily I could sense the indifference the next
time
One you could make all demands come true
The other you is unconcerned and detached
I love both versions
But tell me which you is the real you
The you that loves me unconditionally
Or the you that comes with conditions applied
The you that fills me with joy
Or the one that leaves me in a place of disquiet
Which version would you carry on a day?

Can you let me know beforehand
I will come a little more prepared
I will then decide to carry my heart on my sleeve
Or to protect it with all I have
Let me know what version is the real you
Cause I have fallen for both of you.

The Moment of Truth

I breathe in
Filling my lungs with air
I am in this moment
Living it
Feeling it
I can
See, hear, touch, taste, smell
All my senses align
To this very moment
The moment of truth
The moment of being alive
Not dwelling in the past
Not chasing the future
Not over analysing
The have-beens and the could-bes
Centering myself to the now
Breathing in
Breathing out
Gratitude creeps in
Reminding me
This is what I have
This moment
The only Truth that exists

Come Dance With Me

Come dance with me
Feel the rhythm
Let the music guide you
Let the soul vibrate to the magic
Let your body follow

Come dance with me
Match your steps to mine
In a rhythmic duet
Let the eyes talk to each other
As our smiles light up the sky

Come dance with me
Let us make love through our moves
Telling stories with our bodies
Let the air guide us
As we blend as one with the universe
Creating unforgettable melody

Come dance with me

I Like My Tears

I cry.
Yes, I do.
At the drop of a hat.
And no, I don't cry when I am sad
I mean, I do
But that's not the only time
I cry
I tear up everytime I
Watch a romcom
Hell, I cry when someone tells a heartfelt story in
a reality show
I cry my eyes out when my favourite TV
character dies
I burst into tears when someone else is crying
I am an empath like that
I am moved to tears when my heart is full of
gratitude
My eyes well up when I am happy
And I have a lump in my throat everytime I am
reminiscing good memories

I have to hold back tears every time
I hear a genuine compliment
And I cry buckets when I hear someone's pain
Yes I cry, a lot
I cry when I am happy, sad, angry, confused,
grateful, in love
I like my tears
They make me human
They remind me that I feel
And I am truly thankful for the ability to cry
A tear of joy for everytime
I cry.

My Moon & Yours Too

I looked at the moon in the sky today,
He felt more familiar than before
Like he wasn't a stranger anymore
He was in the sky looking back reassuringly
Witness to my joys, my fears, my tears
And all those victories that I have had
And those yet to come
Extending a hug from beyond the sky
As the whole country embraces this feat
To be able to touch the moon
Even if piggybacking on the courage & belief of
brilliant minds
He is not a stranger anymore
Not just for me
But for a country full of proud people
Who would continue to write poetry, seek love,
break fasts
And share secrets with him
He is my moon & yours too!

www.ingramcontent.com/pod-product-compliance
Lightning Source LLC
LaVergne TN
LVHW021228200726

843509LV00012B/1451